BUENOS AIRES TRAVEL GUIDE

Step-by-Step Travel Companion: From Journey Planning to City
Exploration - Visa, Transportation, Accommodation, Dining,
History, Art, Culture, Landmarks, Events, & More

Arnold Cobbett

TABLE OF CONTENT

INTRODUCTION: WELCOME TO BUENOS AIRES TRAVEL GUIDE

Unlock the vibrant heart of Argentina's capital city with "Buenos Aires Travel Guide," your passport to an unforgettable adventure in one of South America's most captivating destinations. This meticulously crafted travel guide is your key to exploring Buenos Aires like a seasoned traveler, ensuring your journey is not just memorable but extraordinary.

Why "Buenos Aires Travel Guide" Will Become Your Trusted Companion:

Local Insights: Immerse yourself in the rich culture, history, and rhythms of Buenos Aires through the eyes of seasoned local experts. Our guidebook is meticulously researched, providing you with an authentic experience and hidden gems that only insiders know.

Comprehensive Coverage: From the iconic neighborhoods of Palermo and San Telmo to the stunning architecture of Recoleta and the passion of La Boca, we leave no stone unturned. Discover the city's top attractions, hidden treasures, and everything in between.

Culinary Delights: Savor the flavors of Buenos Aires with our expertly curated dining recommendations. Whether you're craving a sizzling asado, mouthwatering empanadas, or the perfect cortado, our guide will lead you to the best culinary experiences.

Cultural Immersion: Dive into the local culture by attending tango shows, exploring art galleries, and mingling with Porteños. Our guide offers tips on how to make the most of your cultural encounters.

Practical Tips: Navigate the city with ease using our insider tips on transportation, accommodations, safety, and more. We've got you covered, from arrival to departure.

Interactive Maps and Itineraries: Visualize your journey with detailed maps and suggested itineraries that cater to various interests and lengths of stay.

Language Assistance: Don't speak Spanish? No problem! We provide essential Spanish phrases and practical language tips to help you communicate effectively during your trip.

Photography Tips: Capture the beauty of Buenos Aires with confidence. Our guide offers photography tips and suggests the best spots for those Instagram-worthy shots.

Traveler Reviews: Benefit from real traveler feedback and recommendations, ensuring your trip is tailored to your preferences.

"Buenos Aires Travel Guide " is not just a travel guide; it's your key to experiencing Buenos Aires in all its glory. With our expert guidance, you'll create memories to cherish for a lifetime. Get ready to embark on an extraordinary journey through the captivating streets, sultry tango rhythms, and mouthwatering flavors of Buenos Aires.

Join the ranks of savvy travelers who have unlocked the secrets of Buenos Aires with "Buenos Aires Travel Guide." Don't miss out on the adventure of a lifetime – order your copy today and start planning your unforgettable trip to the Paris of South America!

1.1 Insights into Buenos Aires Residents' Culture and their Perception of Foreigners

Understanding how Buenos Aires residents perceive foreigners is essential for any visitor looking to have a smooth and culturally enriching experience in this vibrant city. Here are some key insights that can be useful for potential visitors:

Warm Hospitality: Porteños, as Buenos Aires residents are known, are generally warm and welcoming to tourists. They appreciate visitors who show respect for their culture and customs.

Interest in Conversation: Many Porteños are eager to engage in conversations with foreigners, whether it's about politics, soccer (a passion in Argentina), or cultural exchange. Initiating polite conversations with locals can be a great way to connect.

Respect for Personal Space: While Porteños can be friendly, they also value personal space and may find overly familiar behavior uncomfortable. It's important to strike a balance between friendliness and respecting personal boundaries.

Language Matters: Learning a few basic Spanish phrases can go a long way in earning the respect and goodwill of locals. Even if you're not fluent, making an effort to speak the language is greatly appreciated.

Tipping Etiquette: Tipping is customary in Buenos Aires, and it's generally expected in restaurants, cafes, and for services like taxi rides. A 10-15% tip is customary in restaurants, but it's a good idea to check the bill for any included service charge.

Punctuality: Porteños tend to be more relaxed about punctuality compared to some other cultures. Don't be surprised if meetings or appointments start a bit later than scheduled. However, it's still advisable to be on time for tours or group activities.

Dress Code: Buenos Aires is known for its stylish residents. When dining at upscale restaurants or attending cultural events, dressing neatly and stylishly is appreciated. For more casual outings, you can dress comfortably.

Greeting Customs: A kiss on the cheek is a common greeting between friends and acquaintances, but a handshake is also acceptable, especially for formal occasions or when meeting someone for the first time.

Important Tips for Potential Visitors:

Money Matters: Carry cash as credit cards may not be accepted everywhere, especially in smaller establishments. ATMs are widely available for withdrawals.

Safety Precautions: While Buenos Aires is relatively safe, like any major city, it's important to be aware of your surroundings, avoid displaying valuable items, and use reputable taxi services.

Transportation: Buenos Aires has an extensive public transportation system, including buses and the subway (known as the "Subte"). Familiarize yourself with these options to get around efficiently.

Dining Hours: Porteños dine late by some standards. Restaurants often don't open for dinner until 8 or 9 PM. Be prepared for late dining experiences.

Cultural Experiences: Don't miss out on tango shows, local markets, and art exhibitions to immerse yourself in the culture. Also, try the local cuisine, including empanadas, asado, and mate.

Safety at Night: Exercise caution when exploring the city at night, especially in less crowded areas. Stick to well-lit and busy streets.

Weather Awareness: Buenos Aires experiences all four seasons, so check the weather forecast and pack accordingly, especially if you plan to visit during the southern hemisphere's summer (December to February) or winter (June to August).

By being aware of these insights into how Buenos Aires residents perceive foreigners and following these important tips, you can enhance your travel experience and build meaningful connections while exploring this captivating city. Buenos Aires has much to offer, and with the right approach, you'll have an unforgettable visit.

1.2 Navigating the Buenos Aires Financial Landscape

Understanding the currency essentials and monetary matters in Buenos Aires is crucial for a smooth and enjoyable visit. Here are some key tips:

Currency Essentials:

The official currency of Argentina is the Argentine Peso (ARS). Here are some important details about the currency:

Denominations: Argentine Pesos come in both coins and banknotes. Commonly used banknote denominations include 10, 20, 50, 100, 200, 500, and 1,000 pesos. Coins are available in 1, 2, 5, and 10 pesos.

Uses for These Denominations:

Small denomination coins (1, 2, and 5 pesos) are handy for small purchases, like buying snacks or taking public transportation.

10-peso coins can be useful for tipping or making small purchases.

Banknotes are used for larger transactions, such as dining in restaurants, paying for tours, or shopping.

Exchange Options for Foreign Currencies:

ATMs: ATMs are widely available throughout Buenos Aires, and they often provide one of the most favorable exchange rates. Visa and MasterCard are widely accepted, so you can use your debit or credit card to withdraw pesos. Just be aware of any foreign transaction fees your bank may charge.

Currency Exchange Offices (Casas de Cambio): These are common in tourist areas and airports. While convenient, they might offer slightly less favorable exchange rates than ATMs. Compare rates at different exchange offices before making your exchange.

Banks: Many banks in Buenos Aires can exchange foreign currency. However, banking hours can be limited, and you may encounter longer lines, so it's best to use ATMs or exchange offices for convenience.

Useful Denominations and Why:

Carry a mix of small bills and coins, especially for minor expenses like bus fares and tips. Smaller denominations are useful for making exact change.

Larger denominations (100, 200, 500, and 1,000 pesos) are convenient for larger purchases or settling hotel bills.

Keep some small bills and coins handy for purchasing items in local markets or street stalls, where vendors might not have change for larger denominations.

Dual Currencies:

Some businesses in Argentina, especially in tourist areas, may accept US dollars in addition to Argentine Pesos. However, it's not a guaranteed practice, and the exchange rate for using US dollars might not be as favorable as exchanging for pesos. It's advisable to primarily use the local currency, but having a few US dollars on hand as a backup can be helpful.

Additional Tips:

Notify your bank about your travel plans to prevent your credit or debit card from being blocked due to international transactions.

Keep a small amount of US dollars in crisp, clean bills as a backup, but prioritize using pesos.

Be cautious when exchanging money on the street, as scams can occur. Stick to reputable exchange offices and banks.

Familiarize yourself with the current exchange rate to avoid getting shortchanged.

Please note that the currency situation can change over time, so it's essential to check the most recent information before your trip to ensure you have the most up-to-date guidance on money and monetary matters in Buenos Aires.

1.3 The Art of Budget Travel in Buenos Aires

Buenos Aires, the vibrant capital of Argentina, offers an attractive blend of affordability and cosmopolitan living. Here's a breakdown of daily living costs and economic insights that can be helpful to potential tourists:

Accommodation:

Accommodation costs vary widely depending on the neighborhood and type of lodging. Budget travelers can find hostels and guesthouses for as low as $20-50 USD per night.

Mid-range hotels and Airbnb apartments typically range from $70-150 USD per night.

Luxury accommodations can go well above $200 USD per night.

Food and Dining:

Dining out in Buenos Aires can be very affordable. A meal at a local restaurant or cafe might cost around $8-15 USD per person, excluding drinks.

A three-course meal at a mid-range restaurant can range from $20-40 USD.

Grocery shopping for essentials is reasonable, with a week's worth of groceries for one person costing approximately $30-50 USD.

Transportation:

Public transportation is cost-effective, with a single subway or bus ticket costing less than $1 USD.

Taxis are relatively affordable, with rates starting at around $0.50-1 USD per kilometer.

Renting a bike or using ride-sharing apps like Uber are additional transportation options.

Entertainment and Activities:

Cultural activities, such as museum admissions or tango shows, may range from $5-20 USD per person.

Nightlife in Buenos Aires offers a wide range of options. A night out in a bar or club may cost $20-50 USD, including drinks.

Job Availabilities:

For tourists, finding employment in Buenos Aires can be challenging due to visa restrictions. Most tourists visit on a tourist visa, which does not allow for employment.

If you plan to work, it's essential to secure the appropriate work visa or look for opportunities in advance. Teaching English and freelance work are common options for expatriates.

Daily Struggles:

One of the challenges in Buenos Aires is inflation, which can affect prices and the cost of living. The exchange rate can fluctuate, impacting the value of foreign currencies.

Like many big cities, Buenos Aires experiences traffic congestion during rush hours, so plan your commute accordingly.

Petty theft, such as pickpocketing, can occur in crowded areas, so it's essential to be cautious with your belongings.

Useful Tips for Tourists:

Currency Exchange: Use reputable exchange offices or ATMs for currency exchange to get the best rates. Be aware of the official exchange rate versus the black market rate.

Safety: Exercise common-sense safety precautions, such as keeping your belongings secure, avoiding poorly lit areas at night, and being cautious when using ATMs.

Learn Basic Spanish: While many locals in tourist areas speak English, learning some basic Spanish phrases can be incredibly helpful and appreciated.

Local Cuisine: Don't miss trying local specialties like empanadas, asado (Argentine barbecue), and mate (traditional Argentine tea).

Public Transportation: Take advantage of the efficient and cost-effective public transportation system to explore the city.

Cultural Sensitivity: Respect local customs and be mindful of cultural nuances, such as greeting with a kiss on the cheek.

Plan Ahead: Research and plan your itinerary in advance to make the most of your time in Buenos Aires, especially if you have specific attractions or activities in mind.

Buenos Aires is a city of contrasts, offering a unique blend of European elegance and South American flair. By being well-prepared and aware of daily living costs, economic insights, and tips, you can make the most of your visit to this captivating city while staying within your budget and enjoying all it has to offer.

14

2.1 Indispensable Safety Protocols for Discerning Travelers

Buenos Aires is generally a safe city for tourists, but like any major urban center, it's essential to be aware of your surroundings and take precautions to ensure a safe and enjoyable visit. Here are some safety tips and insights to keep in mind:

Safety Records and Police Presence:

Buenos Aires has a relatively low crime rate for a city of its size, and violent crimes against tourists are rare. However, petty crimes like pickpocketing can occur, especially in crowded areas.

The city has a visible police presence, particularly in tourist areas. Law enforcement agencies are generally responsive to reports of incidents involving tourists.

Safety Tips:

Stay in Safe Areas: Choose accommodations in safe neighborhoods like Palermo, Recoleta, or San Telmo. These areas are popular with tourists and generally safer.

Use Reputable Transportation: Opt for licensed taxis or ride-sharing services like Uber. Avoid unmarked or unofficial taxis.

Keep Valuables Secure: Use a money belt or concealed pouch to carry important documents, such as your passport and extra cash. Be discreet with expensive jewelry and electronics.

Avoid Nighttime Solo Adventures: While Buenos Aires is vibrant at night, it's advisable to explore in groups or pairs, especially in less crowded or well-lit areas.

Be Cautious with ATMs: Use ATMs inside banks or secure locations during daylight hours. Be discreet when withdrawing money.

Blend In: Dress casually and avoid displaying excessive wealth. This can help you avoid becoming a target for theft.

Learn Basic Spanish Phrases: Knowing some basic Spanish can be helpful for communication and getting assistance in case of emergencies.

Beware of Scams: Be wary of individuals approaching you with sob stories or "too good to be true" offers. Common scams include the "fake petition," where someone distracts you while an accomplice pickpockets you.

Coping with Beggars: It's common to encounter beggars, especially in tourist areas. You can politely decline or offer food instead of money if you wish to help.

Navigating Challenges:

In case of an emergency or if you're a victim of a crime, contact the Tourist Police (Policía de Turismo) or the general police force (Policía Federal). They are generally responsive and can assist you with language barriers.

Street Dynamics:

Buenos Aires is a bustling city with vibrant street life. Enjoy the lively atmosphere but remain aware of your surroundings. Sidewalks can be uneven, so watch your step.

Local Demonstrations:

Buenos Aires occasionally experiences protests and demonstrations. While they are generally peaceful, it's best to avoid these events to prevent any inadvertent involvement.

Public Transportation:

The public transportation system, including buses and the subway (Subte), is generally safe. However, be cautious of crowded buses and watch your belongings.

Emergency Numbers:

In case of emergency, dial 911 for immediate assistance. For tourist-related issues or assistance, you can call the Tourist Police at +54 11 4346-5748.

Travel Insurance:

Consider purchasing travel insurance that covers medical emergencies, trip cancellations, and theft. It's a wise precaution for any international trip.

By staying vigilant and following these safety tips, you can have a secure and enjoyable experience while exploring the vibrant and culturally rich city of Buenos Aires. Remember that most tourists visit the city without any major incidents, and with the right precautions, you can minimize any potential risks and focus on enjoying your trip.

Chapter 3: Traveler's Essentials

3.1 The Essentials for a Seamless Journey

Preparing and packing for a trip to Buenos Aires requires some thoughtful consideration to ensure a smooth and enjoyable visit. Here's a comprehensive guide to help you pack smartly:

Travel Documents:

Passport and Visa: Ensure your passport is valid for at least six months beyond your planned departure date. Check visa requirements based on your nationality.

Travel Insurance: Carry a copy of your travel insurance policy and contact details in case of emergencies.

Photocopies: Make photocopies of important documents such as your passport, visa, and credit cards. Store these separately from the originals.

Health and Medications:

Prescription Medications: Bring an ample supply of any prescription medications you may need, along with a copy of the prescription itself.

Over-the-Counter Medications: Pack essentials like pain relievers, antacids, allergy medication, and any personal hygiene products.

First Aid Kit: Include band-aids, antiseptic wipes, and any specific medical items you may require.

Hygiene and Personal Care:

Toiletries: Pack travel-sized toiletries such as shampoo, conditioner, soap, toothpaste, and a toothbrush. You can buy more when you arrive.

Sunscreen: Buenos Aires can get quite sunny, so a good quality sunscreen is essential.

Insect Repellent: Depending on the season, insect repellent might be necessary, especially if you plan to explore outdoor areas.

Clothing and Footwear:

Layered Clothing: Buenos Aires experiences various seasons, so pack clothing suitable for the time of year. Lightweight, breathable fabrics are great for summer, while layers are essential for cooler weather.

Comfortable Walking Shoes: Buenos Aires is a walkable city, so bring comfortable walking shoes or sneakers for exploring.

Appropriate Attire: Dress casually but neatly. You might want to pack a slightly dressier outfit for dining at upscale restaurants or attending cultural events.

Electronics and Accessories:

Universal Adapter: Argentina uses Type C and Type I power outlets. A universal adapter will allow you to charge your devices.

Mobile Phone and Charger: Consider getting a local SIM card or an international data plan to stay connected.

Travel Accessories: Items like a portable charger, a power bank, and noise-canceling headphones can enhance your travel experience.

Money and Security:

Money Belt or Hidden Pouch: Keep important documents, extra cash, and credit cards secure with a hidden pouch or money belt.

Anti-Theft Bag: Use a crossbody bag or backpack with anti-theft features like locking zippers and slash-resistant straps.

Travel Guides and Maps:

Guidebooks: Carry a Buenos Aires travel guidebook to help plan your trip and navigate the city. Lonely Planet and Fodor's are popular options.

Maps: Physical maps of the city can be handy, especially for navigating neighborhoods with less reliable cell service.

Additional Tips:

Check the weather forecast for Buenos Aires before packing to ensure you have the appropriate clothing.

Pack a reusable water bottle to stay hydrated while exploring the city.

Consider packing a small daypack or tote bag for carrying essentials during your daily outings.

Keep a copy of your itinerary and important contact numbers in case of emergencies.

Notify your bank of your travel plans to avoid any issues with using your credit or debit cards.

By following these packing and preparation tips, you'll be well-equipped for your journey to Buenos Aires. Remember to pack smart, but also leave some space in your suitcase for souvenirs and treasures you may pick up along the way!

4.1 Navigating Visas, Flights, and Expert Insights

Traveling to Buenos Aires from the United States is an exciting adventure. Here's a step-by-step guide to help you plan your trip:

Visa Requirements and Process:

Visa: For American tourists, Argentina offers a visa-free stay of up to 90 days for tourism purposes. This means you do not need a tourist visa to enter Argentina for short visits. However, your passport must be valid for at least six months beyond your planned departure date.

Booking Flights:

Flight Booking: When booking flights from the United States to Buenos Aires, you have several options. It's advisable to book well in advance for the best fares. Here are some expert tips:

Flexibility: Be flexible with your travel dates. Mid-week flights are often cheaper than weekend departures.

Flight Search Engines: Use flight search engines like Google Flights, Skyscanner, Kayak, or Momondo to compare fares across multiple airlines.

Set Fare Alerts: Consider setting fare alerts to monitor price changes and book when fares are at their lowest.

Airlines: Major U.S. airlines like American, Delta, United, and LATAM operate flights to Buenos Aires. Research and compare prices and services offered by these carriers.

Stopovers: Direct flights from the U.S. to Buenos Aires are available, but flights with one or more stopovers may be more affordable. Consider if you're willing to spend additional time in transit to save money.

Seasonal Variation: Prices can vary seasonally. High season in Buenos Aires is typically during the Southern Hemisphere's summer (December to February).

Cost Considerations:

Budget-Friendly Options: To find the best airfare deals, consider the following:

Off-Peak Travel: Travel during shoulder or off-peak seasons can yield more budget-friendly fares.

Use Fare Comparison Websites: Websites like Skyscanner, Google Flights, and Kayak allow you to compare prices and select the most economical options.

Airlines' Promotions: Keep an eye on airlines' websites and subscribe to fare alerts to catch special promotions and discounts.

Consider Nearby Airports: Sometimes, flying into a nearby airport and taking a domestic flight or bus to Buenos Aires can be cost-effective.

Travel Agents vs. DIY Booking:

4. Booking Method: Whether to use a travel agent or book on your own depends on your preferences and experience.

DIY Booking: Booking your own flights can be more cost-effective and gives you control over your itinerary. Use online tools for research and booking.

Travel Agents: Travel agents can be helpful if you prefer someone else to handle the details, especially for complex itineraries. However, their services may come with additional fees.

Arrival Procedures:

Customs and Immigration: Upon arrival in Buenos Aires, you'll need to go through customs and immigration. Have your passport and a completed customs declaration form ready for inspection.

Airport Transportation: From Ezeiza International Airport (EZE), the main international gateway to Buenos Aires, you can take taxis or pre-arranged airport transfers to your accommodation.

Additional Tips:

Check entry requirements and travel advisories issued by the U.S. Department of State before your trip.

Have a copy of your travel insurance, hotel reservations, and a list of emergency contact numbers with you.

Familiarize yourself with basic Spanish phrases to facilitate communication.

In summary, traveling from the United States to Buenos Aires is a straightforward process for American tourists due to visa-free entry. Booking flights can be cost-effective with careful planning and the use of flight search engines. Whether you book on your own or use a travel agent depends on your preferences and travel style. Be sure to research and compare options to find the best deals for your journey to this vibrant South American destination.

4.2 Demystifying Immigration, Accommodation, and Transportation

Arriving in Buenos Aires from America is a straightforward process, but it's helpful to know what to expect at the airport, immigration, and customs, as well as how to navigate these steps effectively.

Flight Hours:

Flights from the United States to Buenos Aires can vary in duration depending on your departure city. Non-stop flights can take anywhere from 9 to 15 hours, depending on your departure location and the airline.

Immigration and Customs Clearance:

Upon arrival at Buenos Aires' Ezeiza International Airport (EZE), follow the signs to immigration and customs.

If you're an American tourist, you'll typically be granted a 90-day visa-free stay for tourism purposes.

Navigating Immigration Checkpoints:

Immigration Form: Before reaching the immigration checkpoint, you'll be given a form to complete. This form typically includes questions about your purpose of visit, duration of stay, and accommodation details. Make sure to have a pen handy to fill it out.

Immigration Interview: At the immigration checkpoint, an officer may ask questions about your visit. Common questions include:

Purpose of Visit: "What is the purpose of your visit to Argentina?"

Duration of Stay: "How long do you plan to stay in Argentina?"

Accommodation: "Where will you be staying in Buenos Aires?"

Best Responses:

"I'm here for tourism and plan to stay for [number of days]."

Provide the name and address of your accommodation, whether it's a hotel or Airbnb.

Accommodation Arrangements:

Accommodation in Buenos Aires varies from budget-friendly hostels to luxurious hotels and Airbnb rentals. It's advisable to book your accommodation in advance, especially during the peak tourist season (December to February).

Strategizing Hotel Bookings:

Use reputable travel websites and booking platforms like Booking.com, Expedia, or Airbnb to search for accommodation options.

Read reviews from previous guests to ensure the quality of your chosen accommodation.

Consider the location carefully, as different neighborhoods offer different experiences. Palermo, Recoleta, and San Telmo are popular choices among tourists.

Leaving the Airport:

After clearing immigration and customs, you'll exit the airport into the arrival hall.

From Ezeiza International Airport (EZE), you can arrange various transportation options to reach your accommodation:

Cost-Effective Transportation Options:

Taxis: Official airport taxis are readily available. Ensure you take a licensed taxi from the airport taxi stand and agree on a fare with the driver or ask them to use the meter.

Airport Shuttle Services: Shared shuttle services are available and can be cost-effective if you're traveling with a group or want a budget-friendly option.

Public Bus: The "Tienda León" shuttle bus service connects the airport with various neighborhoods in Buenos Aires, including the city center. It's an economical choice, but the journey may take longer due to multiple stops.

Pre-arranged Airport Transfers: Some hotels offer airport transfer services, which can be convenient and provide a hassle-free start to your trip.

Remember to have some Argentine Pesos (ARS) on hand for transportation expenses from the airport, as not all transportation options may accept foreign currency or cards. Buenos Aires is a vibrant city with much to offer, and a smooth arrival process sets the tone for an enjoyable visit.

29

30

Chapter 5: Unveiling Buenos Aires

5.1 A Traveler's Guide to Navigating the City

Navigating Buenos Aires is relatively easy, thanks to a variety of transportation options that cater to both tourists and locals. Here's a comprehensive guide on how to get around the city conveniently:

1. Taxis:

Types of Taxis: Buenos Aires has different types of taxis, including traditional black-and-yellow taxis, remises (private cars available for hire), and radio taxis (dispatched by radio companies).

Fares: Taxi fares are metered and affordable. The initial fare and the per-kilometer rate vary slightly between different types of taxis. The initial fare was around 50-70 Argentine Pesos (ARS), and the per-kilometer rate was approximately 10-15 ARS. Prices may have changed, so it's advisable to check current rates.

2. Ride-Sharing Apps:

Apps like Uber and Cabify operate in Buenos Aires. They can be more convenient and cost-effective than traditional taxis. However, please note that the legality and availability of ride-sharing services may change, so check the current status during your visit.

3. Public Transit:

Subway (Subte): Buenos Aires has a subway system with several lines that can take you to various parts of the city. Fares are reasonable, and the Subte is a fast way to get around.

Buses: The city's extensive bus network covers nearly every corner of Buenos Aires. Fares are affordable, but navigating the bus routes can be challenging for non-Spanish speakers. The "Guía T" is a helpful guidebook that provides bus routes and schedules.

Prepaid SUBE Card: For both the Subte and buses, consider getting a SUBE card, a rechargeable smart card that offers discounted fares and makes using public transit more convenient.

4. Bicycles:

Buenos Aires has a bike-sharing system called "Ecobici," with stations throughout the city. You can register for a card and use it to rent bikes for short trips. It's a fun and eco-friendly way to explore.

5. Walking:

Many of Buenos Aires' neighborhoods, like Palermo and San Telmo, are pedestrian-friendly and perfect for exploring on foot. Wear comfortable shoes and take in the city's unique architecture and culture.

6. Car Rentals:

While it's possible to rent a car, it's generally not recommended for tourists due to the city's traffic congestion, one-way streets, and limited parking. Public transportation and taxis are usually more convenient and cost-effective.

7. Private Car Services:

Some hotels offer private car services or airport transfers, which can be convenient if you prefer door-to-door transportation.

8. Cost Implications:

Transportation costs in Buenos Aires are relatively affordable compared to many other major cities. Taxi fares, public transit, and ride-sharing services offer good value for money.

Tips for Getting Around:

Learn basic Spanish phrases or have a translation app handy for communication with taxi drivers and asking for directions.

Use the SUBE card for convenience and discounts on public transit.

Be aware of pickpocketing in crowded areas, especially on public transportation.

Check the traffic situation before opting for taxis or ride-sharing services during peak hours.

Take advantage of walking and public transit to experience the city's vibrant neighborhoods and culture.

With the variety of transportation options available, you can explore Buenos Aires efficiently and enjoy all that this captivating city has to offer.

5.2 Communication Strategies, Language Fundamentals, and Internet Access

Staying connected while traveling in Buenos Aires is essential for communication with loved ones, navigation, and accessing important information. Here's a guide to help you achieve safe and secure communication:

1. Telecommunications Options:

Local SIM Card: One of the most cost-effective ways to stay connected in Buenos Aires is to purchase a local SIM card. Major providers include Claro, Movistar, and Personal. You can buy SIM cards at kiosks, phone stores, or at the airport. Ensure your phone is unlocked before purchasing a SIM card.

International Roaming: If you prefer to use your home country's SIM card, check with your mobile provider about international roaming packages. However, roaming can be expensive, so be aware of the charges.

2. Phone Booths:

Phone booths, known as "locutorios," are still available in Buenos Aires, but they are becoming less common due to the prevalence of mobile phones. To use a locutorio, you'll need to purchase prepaid calling cards, which are widely available at kiosks.

3. Calling Cards:

Prepaid calling cards can be used with both landlines and mobile phones. To use them, follow the instructions on the card to dial the access number and your PIN, then enter the destination number. Calling cards are available in various denominations and can be a cost-effective way to make international calls.

4. Language Essentials:

Spanish is the official language of Argentina. While many people in Buenos Aires, especially in tourist areas, speak some English, learning basic Spanish phrases can be immensely helpful for effective communication. Consider picking up a phrasebook or using language learning apps to get started.

5. Internet Access:

Internet access is widely available in Buenos Aires. Here are some options:

Wi-Fi: Many hotels, cafes, and restaurants offer free Wi-Fi to customers. Check with your accommodation to see if they provide Wi-Fi in rooms or common areas.

Mobile Data: If you have a local SIM card or an international data plan, you can use mobile data to access the internet on your smartphone. Data speeds are generally good in urban areas.

Internet Cafes: While less common than in the past, there are still internet cafes where you can access the internet for a fee.

6. Cost Implications:

The cost of staying connected in Buenos Aires can vary depending on your choices. Using a local SIM card or Wi-Fi at your accommodation is generally more cost-effective than international roaming.

7. Internet in Hotels:

Many hotels in Buenos Aires, especially mid-range and upscale options, offer free Wi-Fi to guests. Some may charge for high-speed access, so it's a good idea to clarify the terms with your hotel when booking.

8. Internet Speed:

Internet speed in Buenos Aires is generally good, with most places offering high-speed connections suitable for video calls, streaming, and browsing.

By following these tips and using local SIM cards, Wi-Fi, and other available options, you can stay safely connected during your visit to Buenos Aires, ensuring you have access to important information and can easily communicate with loved ones back home. Learning some basic Spanish phrases will also enhance your overall experience and make interactions with locals more enjoyable.

5.3 Buenos Aires Safety Measures and Legal Insights

Ensuring your health and safety during your trip to Buenos Aires is essential for a memorable and trouble-free visit. Here are some important tips and precautions:

1. Local Drug Laws:

Argentina has strict drug laws, and the possession, use, or trafficking of illegal drugs is illegal. This includes substances like cannabis and cocaine. Penalties for drug-related offenses can be severe and may result in imprisonment.

2. Police Conduct:

The police in Buenos Aires generally conduct themselves professionally. While cases of corruption and bribery are relatively rare, it's advisable to be respectful and cooperative when dealing with law enforcement.

If you have any concerns about police behavior, note the officer's badge number and seek assistance from your country's embassy or consulate.

3. Critical Situations and Emergencies:

In case of critical situations or emergencies, here's what to do:

Medical Emergencies: If you have a medical emergency, call 911 or go to the nearest hospital. Buenos Aires has excellent medical facilities and trained healthcare professionals.

Non-Medical Emergencies: If you encounter a non-medical emergency, such as a theft or loss of important documents, contact your country's embassy or consulate for assistance. They can provide guidance and support.

4. Health Precautions:

Buenos Aires is generally safe for tourists, but like any major city, it's important to take health precautions:

Vaccinations: Ensure your routine vaccinations are up to date. Depending on your travel plans, consider vaccinations for diseases like hepatitis A and typhoid.

Water: It's advisable to drink bottled water or use a water purifier to avoid stomach issues.

Food: Enjoy the local cuisine, but be cautious about street food vendors. Stick to restaurants with good hygiene practices.

Sun Protection: Argentina can have strong sun, especially during the summer. Use sunscreen, wear sunglasses, and a hat to protect yourself from sunburn.

Travel Insurance: Purchase comprehensive travel insurance that covers medical emergencies, trip cancellations, and theft. Carry a copy of your policy and contact details.

5. Personal Safety:

To enhance your personal safety:

Stay Aware: Be aware of your surroundings and avoid displaying valuable items like expensive jewelry or electronics.

Secure Belongings: Use hotel safes to store passports, extra cash, and important documents.

Transportation: Choose reputable transportation options, especially for late-night travel.

Walking at Night: While some neighborhoods are safe for nighttime walks, exercise caution in less well-lit areas.

6. Language Barrier:

While many people in tourist areas speak some English, it's helpful to learn basic Spanish phrases. This can facilitate communication and make your interactions with locals more enjoyable.

7. Seeking Help:

If you need assistance or information, consider contacting your country's embassy or consulate in Buenos Aires. They can provide guidance on various matters, including legal assistance, lost documents, and medical referrals.

By following these health and safety tips and staying informed about local laws and customs, you can enjoy your visit to Buenos Aires with confidence, knowing that you are well-prepared for any situation that may arise.

Chapter 6: Celebrating Diversity and Inclusion

6.1 Understanding Local Attitudes Towards Sex and Legal Aspects in Buenos Aires

Buenos Aires is a cosmopolitan and liberal city with a diverse population. While attitudes toward sex in Buenos Aires are generally open-minded and accepting, it's essential for visitors to respect local customs and be aware of legal aspects related to sexual conduct and relationships.

Legal Aspects of Having Sex with Locals:

The legal age of consent for sexual activity in Argentina is typically 13 years old. However, there are some exceptions and legal intricacies regarding sexual relationships with individuals under 18. It is crucial to be aware of these laws and regulations.

Sexual activity involving minors under the age of 13 is considered a criminal offense and is subject to severe penalties.

It's essential to ensure that any sexual activity is consensual and with individuals who are of legal age to avoid legal consequences.

Prostitution and Related Issues:

Prostitution is legal in Argentina, but it is regulated at the municipal level. The legal age for engaging in sex work is 18.

Prostitution laws can vary by locality, so it's essential to be aware of the specific regulations in Buenos Aires if you intend to engage in or seek the services of sex workers.

While prostitution itself is legal, related activities, such as operating brothels or pimping, may be illegal. Always exercise discretion and caution in this regard.

Visitor Awareness:

Visitors should be respectful of local customs and practices, including those related to sexual conduct.

Practice safe and consensual sexual activity. Use protection and communicate openly with your partner.

Understand the legal framework and age of consent laws in Argentina to avoid any potential legal issues.

Buenos Aires is known for its vibrant nightlife and open-minded culture, but it's essential for visitors to exercise responsible behavior and adhere to local laws and regulations. Always prioritize consent, safety, and respect when engaging in any sexual activity, whether with locals or fellow travelers.

6.2 Buenos Aires LGBTQ Travel

Legal and Social Aspects of LGBTQ Travel in Buenos Aires for American Visitors and Tourists:

Buenos Aires is known for its open and welcoming attitude towards the LGBTQ+ community. As a popular LGBTQ+ destination in South America, the city offers a vibrant and inclusive environment for travelers. Here's what you need to know:

Legal Rights:

Argentina has been at the forefront of LGBTQ+ rights in South America. In 2010, Argentina became the first country in the region to legalize same-sex marriage, allowing LGBTQ+ couples to marry and adopt children.

Discrimination based on sexual orientation is prohibited by law, and LGBTQ+ individuals have legal protections against discrimination in various areas of life.

Social Acceptance:

Buenos Aires is known for its LGBTQ+-friendly neighborhoods, such as San Telmo, Palermo, and Recoleta, which are home to LGBTQ+ bars, clubs, and businesses.

The city hosts several LGBTQ+ events and pride celebrations throughout the year, including the Buenos Aires LGBTQ+ Pride Parade (Marcha del Orgullo LGBTQ+) in November.

Nightlife and Entertainment:

Buenos Aires has a thriving LGBTQ+ nightlife scene, with numerous bars and clubs catering to different tastes. Palermo is particularly well-known for its LGBTQ+-friendly nightlife.

The annual "La Marcha de las Putas" event celebrates LGBTQ+ diversity and visibility with music, performances, and a colorful parade.

Hotels and Accommodations:

Many hotels in Buenos Aires are LGBTQ+-friendly and welcome all guests regardless of sexual orientation or gender identity. Some may even offer LGBTQ+ packages or promotions.

Local LGBTQ+ Organizations:

Organizations like the Argentine Homosexual Community (Comunidad Homosexual Argentina - CHA) and Diversity Buenos Aires provide resources and support for LGBTQ+ individuals and travelers.

Safety Considerations:

Buenos Aires is generally safe for LGBTQ+ travelers. However, as with any international travel, it's essential to exercise standard precautions and be aware of your surroundings.

Language and Communication:

While many locals in Buenos Aires speak some English, it can be helpful to know some basic Spanish phrases. Learning a few local LGBTQ+ terms and phrases can also enhance your experience and communication.

Medical Care:

Buenos Aires has a comprehensive healthcare system that includes LGBTQ+ healthcare services. If you have specific healthcare needs, research LGBTQ+-friendly healthcare providers in the city.

Respect for Local Customs:

Buenos Aires is a diverse and cosmopolitan city, but it's still important to be respectful of local customs and practices. PDA (public displays of affection) is generally acceptable in LGBTQ+-friendly neighborhoods but may draw more attention in other areas.

Buenos Aires is a fantastic destination for LGBTQ+ travelers, offering a warm and accepting environment. By being informed and respectful, you can fully enjoy the city's vibrant LGBTQ+ culture and explore its many attractions, events, and welcoming communities.

Chapter 7: Health and Well-Being

7.1 Medication, Hospitals, and Optimal Well-Being

Before traveling to Buenos Aires, it's essential for American tourists to be prepared for potential health concerns and ensure they have necessary medications on hand. Here are some recommendations and tips:

Essential Medications:

Prescription Medications: Ensure you have an ample supply of any prescription medications you regularly take. Carry them in their original packaging, and have a copy of your prescription handy.

Over-the-Counter Medications: Pack over-the-counter medications for common ailments such as pain relievers, antacids, allergy medication, and any personal hygiene products.

First Aid Kit: Include items like band-aids, antiseptic wipes, pain relievers, and any specific medical items you may require.

Common Health Concerns:

Traveler's Diarrhea: It's not uncommon for travelers to experience gastrointestinal issues due to changes in diet and water. Stick to bottled water, avoid ice in drinks, and eat at reputable restaurants to minimize the risk.

Sunburn: Buenos Aires can be sunny, so use sunscreen and protect yourself from excessive sun exposure.

Mosquito-Borne Illnesses: Depending on the season, mosquito-borne illnesses like dengue and Zika can be a concern. Use insect repellent and consider wearing long sleeves and pants in areas with a high mosquito presence.

Healthcare in Buenos Aires:

Hospitals: Buenos Aires has excellent healthcare facilities, including public and private hospitals. Some reputable private hospitals in the city include Hospital Alemán, Hospital Italiano, and Hospital Británico.

Costs: Medical costs in Buenos Aires are generally lower than in the United States. However, the specific cost of medical care can vary depending on the treatment required. It's advisable to have travel insurance that covers medical emergencies to avoid unexpected expenses.

Tips for Staying Healthy:

Water: Drink bottled water or use a water purifier to avoid stomach issues.

Food: While Buenos Aires offers delicious cuisine, be cautious about street food vendors. Choose restaurants with good hygiene practices.

Safety: Exercise caution when walking at night, especially in less well-lit areas.

Sun Protection: Use sunscreen, wear sunglasses, and a hat to protect yourself from sunburn.

Insurance: Purchase comprehensive travel insurance that covers medical emergencies, trip cancellations, and lost belongings.

Local Customs: Be mindful of local customs and practices, such as the siesta (afternoon nap) when many businesses close temporarily.

Language: Learn some basic Spanish phrases or have a translation app handy for communication.

Vaccinations: Ensure your routine vaccinations are up to date and consider vaccinations for diseases like hepatitis A and typhoid depending on your travel plans.

Hand Sanitizer: Carry hand sanitizer for use when soap and water are not readily available.

By being prepared with essential medications, staying informed about common health concerns, and following these health tips, American tourists can enjoy their trip to Buenos Aires while minimizing health-related risks and ensuring a safe and healthy travel experience.

8.1 Diverse Accommodation Options with Comprehensive Details

Here is a list of accommodation choices in Buenos Aires, including hotels and private residences, along with pricing, tips, and contact information. Please note that prices and availability may vary, so it's advisable to check with the establishments directly for the most up-to-date information:

Hotels:

Alvear Palace Hotel (5-Star)

Address: Av. Alvear 1891, C1129AAA CABA, Argentina

Pricing: Luxury; rates vary by room type and season.

Contact: reservations@alvearpalace.com, +54 11 4808-2100

Hotel Pulitzer (4-Star)

Address: Maipú 907, C1006ACM CABA, Argentina

Pricing: Mid-range; rates vary by room type and season.

Contact: info@hotelpulitzer.com.ar, +54 11 4316-0800

Hotel Tango de Mayo (4-Star)

Address: Av. de Mayo 1396, C1085ABQ CABA, Argentina

Pricing: Mid-range; rates vary by room type and season.

Contact: info@hoteltangodemayo.com.ar, +54 11 5263-7400

Hostel Suites Florida (Budget)

Address: Florida 328, C1005AAH CABA, Argentina

Pricing: Budget-friendly; dormitory and private room options available.

Contact: info@hostelsuitesflorida.com, +54 11 4311-5723

Private Residences (Airbnb):

Palermo Loft with Terrace

Address: Palermo, Buenos Aires, Argentina

Pricing: Varies by season and length of stay; typically budget-friendly.

Listing Link: Palermo Loft with Terrace

Recoleta Apartment with Pool

Address: Recoleta, Buenos Aires, Argentina

Pricing: Mid-range; suitable for families.

Listing Link: Recoleta Apartment with Pool

San Telmo Studio

Address: San Telmo, Buenos Aires, Argentina

Pricing: Budget-friendly; great for solo travelers or couples.

Listing Link: San Telmo Studio

Tips:

Consider booking well in advance, especially during the high tourist season (December to February).

Look for package deals and promotions that some hotels offer.

Check guest reviews and ratings on travel websites or platforms like TripAdvisor or Booking.com for additional insights.

Be aware of check-in/check-out times and cancellation policies.

Please note that the prices mentioned here are indicative and subject to change based on availability and seasonal variations. Always contact the accommodation providers directly or visit their websites for the most accurate and up-to-date pricing information. Buenos Aires offers a wide range of lodging options to suit different budgets and preferences, ensuring a comfortable stay for American tourists.

54

9.1 Culinary Must-Visits: The Top Dining Experiences

Buenos Aires is a culinary paradise known for its diverse and flavorful cuisine. From traditional Argentine steakhouses to trendy fusion restaurants, the city offers a wide range of dining options to satisfy every palate. Here's a comprehensive guide to dining in Buenos Aires:

Must-Visit Restaurants:

Don Julio

Cuisine: Argentine Steakhouse (Parrilla)

Address: Guatemala 4699, C1414BJM CABA, Argentina

Pricing: Moderate to high, with steak dishes being the highlight.

Tip: Try the renowned Argentine steak, empanadas, and Malbec wine.

El Preferido de Palermo

Cuisine: Argentine-European Fusion

Address: Jorge Luis Borges 2108, C1425HOB CABA, Argentina

Pricing: Moderate to high; offers creative dishes with a focus on local ingredients.

Tip: Don't miss the "milanesa" or the homemade pasta.

Tegui (Reservation-Only)

Cuisine: Modern Argentine

Address: Costa Rica 5852, C1414BTJ CABA, Argentina

Pricing: High-end; tasting menu experience.

Tip: This Michelin-starred restaurant offers an intimate dining experience with a set tasting menu.

La Brigada

Cuisine: Argentine Steakhouse (Parrilla)

Address: Estados Unidos 465, C1101ABK CABA, Argentina

Pricing: Moderate to high; famous for its steaks.

Tip: Order a "bife de chorizo" or ribeye steak.

Local Cuisines to Try:

Asado: Argentine barbecue is a must-try. Savor cuts like "bife de chorizo" (sirloin) and "matambre" (flank steak) cooked on a parrilla (grill).

Empanadas: These savory pastries come in various fillings like beef, chicken, ham, and cheese. You can find them at bakeries and specialized empanada shops.

Milanesa: Similar to a breaded cutlet, often made with beef or chicken. It's a delicious comfort food.

Provoleta: Melted provolone cheese with herbs and spices, often served as an appetizer.

Dulce de Leche: A sweet caramel spread used in desserts and pastries.

Dining Experiences:

Street Food: Buenos Aires offers street food delights like choripán (sausage sandwich), lomito (steak sandwich), and panchos (hot dogs). You can find street food vendors in popular neighborhoods.

Hotel Dining: Many hotels offer on-site dining options with a range of cuisines, from local Argentine to international dishes.

Cafés and Bakeries: Buenos Aires is famous for its cafés and bakeries where you can enjoy medialunas (croissants), coffee, and pastries. Try Café Tortoni, one of the oldest cafés in the city.

Pricing:

Dining prices can vary widely. Street food and local eateries are budget-friendly, while upscale restaurants and those in touristy areas tend to be more expensive.

A budget traveler can expect to spend around $10-20 USD for a meal, while mid-range dining might cost $20-50 USD per person. High-end dining experiences can exceed $100 USD per person.

Tips:

Make reservations at popular restaurants, especially during peak dining hours.

Don't forget to try Argentine wines, especially Malbec.

Tipping is customary, and 10-15% is generally considered appropriate.

Buenos Aires offers an exciting culinary journey for visitors, from traditional Argentine classics to innovative fusion cuisine. Exploring the local flavors and dining scene is a delightful part of the Buenos Aires experience.

10.1 Landmarks and Essential Destinations for the Discerning Traveler

Buenos Aires, the vibrant capital of Argentina, offers a rich tapestry of cultural, historical, and architectural attractions. From iconic landmarks to charming neighborhoods, here's a detailed guide to some must-see points of interest in Buenos Aires:

1. Recoleta Cemetery:

Address: Junín 1760, C1113 AAB, Buenos Aires, Argentina

Remarkable Feature: This famous cemetery is known for its elaborate mausoleums, including the final resting place of Eva Perón (Evita). The cemetery is like an outdoor museum with intricate sculptures and artistry.

2. Teatro Colón (Colon Theater):

Address: Cerrito 628, C1012 CABA, Buenos Aires, Argentina

Remarkable Feature: One of the world's top opera houses, Teatro Colón is renowned for its opulent architecture and exceptional acoustics. Take a guided tour or attend a performance.

3. La Casa Rosada (The Pink House):

Address: Balcarce 50, C1064 CABA, Buenos Aires, Argentina

Remarkable Feature: The presidential palace is famous for its pink façade. Visit the Plaza de Mayo in front, where significant historic events have taken place.

4. San Telmo Neighborhood:

Remarkable Feature: Known for its cobblestone streets, colonial architecture, and vibrant arts scene. Don't miss the San Telmo Market on Sundays for antiques and artisan goods.

5. La Boca Neighborhood:

Remarkable Feature: Colorful Caminito Street with its vibrant buildings and street art. Visit the Boca Juniors stadium for a taste of Argentine soccer culture.

6. Palermo Neighborhood:

Remarkable Feature: A trendy area with parks, hip bars, and restaurants. Explore the Bosques de Palermo (Palermo Woods) and the Rose Garden (Rosedal).

7. Museo Nacional de Bellas Artes (National Museum of Fine Arts):

Address: Av. del Libertador 1473, C1425AAA CABA, Buenos Aires, Argentina

Remarkable Feature: Home to an impressive collection of European and Argentine art, including works by Goya, Van Gogh, and local artists.

**8. Puerto Madero:

Remarkable Feature: A modern waterfront district with upscale dining, sleek architecture, and the iconic Puente de la Mujer (Women's Bridge).

**9. Obelisco (Obelisk):

Address: Av. 9 de Julio, C1073ABA CABA, Buenos Aires, Argentina

Remarkable Feature: This iconic landmark is located in the heart of Buenos Aires and is a symbol of the city.

**10. Tigre and the Delta:

- Remarkable Feature: A short trip from the city, Tigre is famous for its picturesque delta with islands, rivers, and boat tours. A relaxing escape from the urban hustle.

Directions from the Airport (Ezeiza - Ministro Pistarini International Airport):

The airport is about 22 miles (35 km) southwest of Buenos Aires.

The easiest way to reach the city is by taxi or pre-arranged airport transfer. The journey takes approximately 45 minutes to an hour, depending on traffic.

Buenos Aires is a city of culture, history, and diversity, offering countless attractions to explore. From the elegant streets of Recoleta to the lively neighborhoods of San Telmo and La Boca, there's something to captivate every traveler's interest in this remarkable city.

Comprehensive Overview of Buenos Aires, Argentina

Geography:

Location: Buenos Aires is located in eastern Argentina, along the southeastern coast of South America, on the western shore of the Río de la Plata estuary.

Climate: Buenos Aires has a temperate climate with distinct seasons. Summers (December to February) are warm and humid, while winters (June to August) are mild and relatively dry. Rainfall is moderate throughout the year.

Coordinates:

Coordinates: 34°36′33″S 58°22′47″W

Elevation:

Elevation Range: The elevation in Buenos Aires varies between sea level along the coast to about 25 meters (82 feet) above sea level in some parts of the city.

Average Elevation: The average elevation in the city is approximately 10 meters (33 feet) above sea level.

Administration:

City Government: Buenos Aires is governed by a Mayor, with the current mayor being Horacio Rodríguez Larreta.

Provincial Government: Buenos Aires is both a city and a province, with its own provincial government, known as the

Autonomous City of Buenos Aires (Ciudad Autónoma de Buenos Aires).

National Government: It also houses the national government institutions, including the Argentine National Congress and the presidential residence, Casa Rosada.

Police Force: The city's law enforcement is managed by the Buenos Aires City Police (Policía de la Ciudad de Buenos Aires).

Subdivisions:

Buenos Aires is divided into 15 administrative communes, each with its own local government.

Total Area:

Total Area: The total land area of Buenos Aires City is approximately 203 square kilometers (78.5 square miles).

Population (2021):

Total Population: As of 2021, Buenos Aires City has a population of approximately 2,890,151 residents.

Density: The city has a population density of around 14,230 people per square kilometer (36,800 per square mile).

Time Zone:

Time Zone: Buenos Aires operates in the Argentina Standard Time zone (ART), which is UTC-3. Argentina does not observe daylight saving time.

INSEE/Postal Code:

INSEE Code: Buenos Aires does not have an INSEE code, as it is not in France.

Postal Codes: The postal codes in Buenos Aires City typically start with "C1" or "C2."

History:

Origins: Buenos Aires was originally inhabited by indigenous peoples before the Spanish founded it in 1536. It later became a significant trading port.

Colonial and Independence Era: It played a crucial role in the struggle for Argentine independence from Spanish colonial rule.

19th and 20th Centuries: Buenos Aires continued to grow and modernize, becoming a cultural and economic center of South America.

Recent History: In more recent history, the city faced economic challenges but has continued to develop as a major global city.

Cityscape:

Urbanism and Architecture: Buenos Aires features a mix of architectural styles, from colonial and Beaux-Arts to modernist and contemporary.

Housing: The city has a diverse range of housing options, including historic apartments, modern condominiums, and suburban residences.

Suburbs: The Greater Buenos Aires area includes suburbs known as the "conurbano," which vary in terms of socio-economic status and development.

Demographics:

Migration: Buenos Aires is home to a diverse population, with immigrants from across Europe, Asia, and the Middle East.

Religion: The city is predominantly Roman Catholic but is also home to various religious communities, including Jewish, Muslim, and Protestant.

Economy:

Employment and Income: Buenos Aires boasts a diverse economy, with sectors such as finance, technology, agriculture, and creative industries contributing significantly.

Tourism: The city is a major tourist destination, known for its tango music, cultural attractions, and vibrant culinary scene.

Culture:

Arts: Buenos Aires has a rich artistic history, with contributions to literature, painting, music, and dance. Tango, in particular, originated here.

Museums: The city is home to renowned museums, including the Museo Nacional de Bellas Artes and Museo de Arte Latinoamericano de Buenos Aires (MALBA).

Theatre: Buenos Aires is a hub for theater, with venues like the Teatro Colón and the historic Teatro Cervantes.

Literature: The city has been the inspiration for many famous writers, including Jorge Luis Borges.

Music: Tango music and folklore are integral to Buenos Aires' cultural identity.

Cinema: Buenos Aires has a thriving film culture and hosts festivals like the Buenos Aires International Festival of Independent Cinema (BAFICI).

Cuisine: Argentine cuisine, including famous beef dishes like asado, is celebrated. Parrillas (steakhouses) and cafés are common dining spots.

Fashion: The city is known for its fashion scene, with design districts like Palermo Soho and fashion weeks.

Infrastructure:

Transportation: Buenos Aires has an extensive public transportation system, including buses, subways, and commuter trains.

Airports: The city is served by two international airports: Ministro Pistarini International Airport (Ezeiza) and Aeroparque Jorge Newbery.

Roads: A network of roads and highways connects Buenos Aires to the rest of Argentina.

Ports: The city has a significant port along the Río de la Plata.

International Relations:

Diplomacy: Buenos Aires hosts various international organizations and embassies and plays a role in international diplomacy.

Twin Cities: The city has twin city relationships with several global metropolises, fostering cultural and economic ties.

Buenos Aires, with its rich history, diverse culture, and dynamic economy, stands as a captivating global city on the southeastern coast of South America. Its fusion of European and Latin American influences makes it a unique and vibrant destination for visitors from around the world.

A Calendar of Seasonal Events and Festivals

January:

Feria de Mataderos (Mataderos Fair): This folk festival celebrates Argentine traditions, with music, dance, crafts, and regional food. Tourists can enjoy the lively atmosphere and shop for souvenirs.

Tango Buenos Aires Festival and Dance World Cup: A world-renowned tango festival that includes dance performances, competitions, and tango classes. Attendees can witness the passion of Argentine tango.

February:

Carnaval Porteño (Buenos Aires Carnival): A vibrant celebration with colorful parades, live music, and dancers in elaborate costumes. The carnival takes place in various neighborhoods, including San Telmo and Barracas.

March:

International Women's Day: While not a festival, it's a significant day with various events and marches in support of gender equality.

Lollapalooza Argentina: A major music festival featuring international and local artists, spanning various genres like rock, pop, and electronic music.

April:

Feria del Libro (Buenos Aires International Book Fair): A literary extravaganza attracting authors, publishers, and book enthusiasts. Tourists can explore a vast selection of books, attend lectures, and meet authors.

Semana Santa (Holy Week): While Buenos Aires isn't known for extravagant Holy Week celebrations, you can attend special masses and processions at historic churches.

May:

Dia de la Revolucion de Mayo (May Revolution Day): Celebrated on May 25th, this national holiday marks the start of the Argentine War of Independence. Tourists can witness traditional parades and performances around the city.

Feria de Mataderos (Mataderos Fair): The folk festival continues, offering tourists another chance to experience Argentine culture.

June:

Festival Internacional de Jazz de Buenos Aires: Jazz enthusiasts can enjoy performances by renowned artists at various venues across the city.

Dia del Amigo (Friendship Day): A day to celebrate friendships, often spent with friends at restaurants, bars, or cafes.

July:

Feria Internacional del Libro Infantil y Juvenil (International Children and Young Adults Book Fair): A literary event focused on children's and young adult literature, featuring book sales, workshops, and storytelling sessions.

Fiesta del Bicentenario de la Independencia (Independence Bicentennial): Celebrated on July 9th, this national holiday marks Argentina's independence from Spain. Tourists can enjoy patriotic parades and fireworks.

August:

Día del Niño (Children's Day): A Day dedicated to children, often celebrated with family outings and special events at parks and museums.

Tango Buenos Aires Festival and Dance World Cup: The tango festival continues, with more opportunities to witness this passionate dance form.

September:

Feria Masticar: A gourmet food fair where tourists can savor Argentine cuisine, including empanadas, asado, and local wines. It's a gastronomic delight.

Noche de los Museos (Night of the Museums): Buenos Aires' museums stay open late, and entry is often free. Tourists can explore the city's cultural institutions after dark.

October:

Buenos Aires International Film Festival (Festival Internacional de Cine de Buenos Aires - BAFICI): Film enthusiasts can attend screenings of local and international films.

Oktoberfest Buenos Aires: While not as famous as its German counterpart, this beer festival offers beer tastings, live music, and traditional German food.

November:

Feria de Artesanos de Plaza Francia (Plaza Francia Artisans Fair): Tourists can browse and purchase unique handcrafted goods and art from local artisans.

Feria de Mataderos (Mataderos Fair): The folk festival continues, providing another opportunity for tourists to immerse themselves in Argentine culture.

December:

Christmas in Buenos Aires: Tourists can experience the festive atmosphere with Christmas lights, decorations, and holiday markets, particularly in neighborhoods like Recoleta and Palermo.

New Year's Eve (Nochevieja): Locals celebrate with fireworks, parties, and gatherings. Puerto Madero and Costanera Sur offer great spots to watch the fireworks over the river.

Please note that event dates and details may change from year to year, so it's advisable to check local event listings and tourist information closer to your visit to Buenos Aires for the most up-to-date information. Buenos Aires offers a diverse range of festivals and events throughout the year, ensuring that tourists can immerse themselves in the city's rich culture and traditions.

Shopping and Nightlife Recommendations in Buenos Aires

Shopping in Buenos Aires:

Buenos Aires offers a diverse shopping experience, from high-end boutiques to vibrant street markets. Here are some shopping recommendations for tourists:

Avenida Santa Fe: This bustling avenue is known for its upscale shops and department stores. You can find international and local brands, including clothing, accessories, and electronics.

Palermo Soho: This trendy neighborhood is a shopping paradise for fashion enthusiasts. It's dotted with boutique stores, designer shops, and unique concept stores. Explore Calle Thames and surrounding streets for fashion finds.

San Telmo Market: Held in the historic San Telmo neighborhood, this market offers a mix of antiques, artisanal goods, and vintage clothing. Don't forget to haggle for unique treasures.

Feria de Mataderos: This folk market is a cultural experience where you can shop for traditional Argentine crafts, textiles, and regional products. Enjoy live music, dance performances, and local food.

Recoleta:

Recoleta Mall (Buenos Aires Design): A mall dedicated to design and decor, featuring upscale stores and design showrooms.

Feria de Artesanos de Plaza Francia: This artisan fair in Plaza Francia offers handmade jewelry, leather goods, and more. It's a great place to find souvenirs.

Florida Street: A pedestrian shopping street in the heart of the city. You'll find a mix of stores, from international chains to local boutiques. Keep an eye out for leather goods.

La Boca: Caminito Street in La Boca is famous for its colorful buildings and street art. It's a great place to buy local art, crafts, and tango memorabilia.

Designer Outlets: Head to outlet malls like Distrito Arcos and Soleil Premium Outlet for discounted designer brands.

Leather Goods: Argentina is known for its high-quality leather products. Look for leather jackets, bags, and shoes in various markets and boutiques.

Nightlife in Buenos Aires:

Buenos Aires comes alive at night with a vibrant nightlife scene that caters to various tastes. Here are some nightlife recommendations for tourists:

Tango Shows: Buenos Aires is the birthplace of tango, and tourists can enjoy captivating tango shows at venues like Café de los Angelitos, El Querandi, and Senor Tango.

Palermo Nightclubs: Palermo is the hub of nightlife in Buenos Aires. You'll find a wide range of bars, clubs, and lounges. Some popular spots include Rosebar, Kika, and Niceto Club.

San Telmo: The historic San Telmo neighborhood has a thriving nightlife scene. Explore its bars, live music venues, and Milongas (tango dance halls).

Puerto Madero: This upscale waterfront district offers fine dining restaurants, stylish bars, and nightclubs with views of the river.

Cafés and Speakeasies: Buenos Aires has a café culture, and many cafés transform into lively bars in the evening. Look for speakeasies hidden behind unmarked doors, such as Florería Atlántico.

La Bomba de Tiempo: Experience a unique percussion show at La Bomba de Tiempo, where drummers create an electrifying atmosphere every Monday night.

Late-Night Dining: Buenos Aires is known for its late dining hours. You can enjoy traditional Argentine dishes at parrillas (steakhouses) well into the night.

Rooftop Bars: Enjoy a cocktail with a view at one of the city's rooftop bars. Some options include the Fierro Hotel rooftop and the Alvear Icon Hotel's Sky Bar.

Themed Bars: Explore themed bars like Frank's Bar, a hidden Prohibition-style speakeasy, and Victoria Brown Bar, known for its eclectic decor and craft cocktails.

Plaza Serrano: This square in Palermo becomes a hub of nightlife in the evenings. It's a great place to enjoy drinks, live music, and the local atmosphere.

Remember that nightlife in Buenos Aires starts late, with many venues opening around midnight and staying open until the early hours of the morning. Whether you're into tango, live music, or dancing the night away, Buenos Aires has something for every type of nightlife enthusiast.

Made in the USA
Las Vegas, NV
22 October 2023

79537779R00050